Marylène Madou
Prints & Patterns

Marylène Madou

Prints & Patterns

Prepare to forget that naive is a dirty word.
Come a little closer.
Then leaf through this book.
Let it tell you about the birds and the bees, vibrant purple,
dashing parrots, and moving brush strokes.
Stop at a random page.
Take a look. Closer. Closer. There.
What just stung?
Was there a sea urchin hiding between the waving seaweed
or did the snakes catch up with you?

Préparez-vous à oublier que la naïveté est un gros mot.
Approchez-vous un peu plus.
Puis feuilletez ce livre.
Laissez-le vous parler des oiseaux et des abeilles, du violet
vibrant, des perroquets fringants et des coups de pinceau
en mouvement.
Arrêtez-vous sur une page aléatoire.
Regardez. Rapprochez. Rapprochez encore. Là.
Qu'est-ce qui vient de piquer?
Y avait-il un oursin caché entre les algues ondulantes ou
les serpents vous ont-ils rattrapé?

Prints & Patterns Introduction

Marylène Madou's *Prints & Patterns* stretches in different directions. A trigger for these dreamy, brimful and inviting images lay in London. Hungry for new impressions, the Belgian print designer moved to the English capital and soaked up the diversity the city had to offer. From historical fabric archives, over botanical gardens to contemporary street styles, it all left its trace in her imagination. She is also intrigued by old-fashioned representations of reality and actively collects old illustrated books. Such mediated looks are an important factor to her kaleidoscopic look on things: nature is a constant inspiration, but Marylène's attention is more likely to be drawn by a picture of a flower on a vase, than by an actual flower in a vase. Just like she prefers a day surrounded by taxidermy collections to a trip to the forest.

In this sense, *Prints & Patterns* is a look over the shoulder. This book is the result of five years of colourful explosions, meticulous design and eclectic inspirations, balancing at the tipping point of art and applied design. Although it can be read in any way you prefer, it is divided into five categories – the top five recurring subjects on Marylène Madou's drawing stand:
Animals & Living Creatures
Flowers & Foliage
Fruits & Vegetables
Objects & People
Abstract & Geometric
It is the starting point of a timeless personal archive in which each design can follow its own thread. For they can turn into anything – something to wear, something to frame, something to live with, something to wonder over.

And so, *Prints & Patterns* is also a look forward. The buzzing universe that is before you does not exist. Yet. Marylène Madou does not draw the world as it is, but the world as she wants it to be. Even though the techniques and styles vary, you will recognise the steady hand of a creative mind in the use of saturated colours, an eye for detail and the sparkling attitude that glows from every print – naive with a punch. Each drawing is a colourful step closer to bringing the colliding images out of the designer's head, and into the world.

–Sofie Gielis

Les *Prints & Patterns* de Marylène Madou se répandent dans différentes directions. Un des déclencheurs de ces images rêveuses, débordantes et invitantes se trouvait à Londres. Avide de nouvelles impressions, la désigneuse d'impression belge s'est installée dans la capitale anglaise et s'est imprégnée de la diversité que la ville avait à offrir. Des archives historiques de tissus, en passant par les jardins botaniques, aux styles de rue contemporains, tout cela a laissé sa trace dans son imagination. Elle est également intriguée par les représentations démodées de la réalité et collectionne activement de vieux livres illustrés. De tels regards médiatisés composent un élément important de son regard kaléidoscopique sur les choses: la nature est une source constante d'inspiration, mais l'attention de Marylène est plus susceptible d'être attirée par l'image d'une fleur sur un vase, que par la fleur réelle dans ce même vase. Tout comme elle préfère une journée entourée de collections de taxidermie à un voyage en forêt.

En ce sens, *Prints & Patterns* est un regard par-dessus l'épaule. Ce livre est le résultat de cinq ans d'explosions de couleurs fourmillantes, de design méticuleux et d'inspirations éclectiques, s'équilibrant au point de basculement de l'art et du design appliqué. Bien qu'il puisse être lu de la manière que vous préférez, le livre est divisé en cinq catégories — les cinq principaux sujets récurrents sur la planche à dessin de Marylène Madou:
Animaux & Créatures Vivantes
Fleurs & Feuillage
Fruits & Légumes
Objets & Personnes
Abstrait & Géométrique
C'est le point de départ d'une archive personnelle intemporelle dans laquelle chaque design peut suivre son propre fil. Car celui peut se transformer en n'importe quoi – quelque chose à porter, quelque chose à encadrer, quelque chose avec lequel vivre, quelque chose de quoi s'émerveiller.

Et donc, *Prints & Patterns* est également un regard vers l'avenir. L'univers bourdonnant qui est devant vous n'existe pas. Encore. Marylène Madou ne dessine pas le monde tel qu'il est, mais le monde tel qu'elle veut qu'il soit. Même si les techniques et les styles varient, vous reconnaîtrez la main ferme d'un esprit créatif dans l'utilisation de couleurs saturées, le souci du détail et le caractère pétillant qui rayonne dans chaque image – naïve avec un coup de poing. Chaque dessin est un pas coloré vers la sortie, hors de la tête de la désigneuse, d'images en collision, en direction du monde.

Animals & Living Creatures

How the animal kingdom is represented in historical scientific prints,
interesting embroidery of creatures on an old Indian tablecloth, or perhaps a
simple bird in the garden: providing for endless inspiration, living elements
around us are constantly reinterpreted into new printable imagery.

KOI POND CIRCLE JAPAN

2017

Watercolour, black pigment fineliner, gouache paint, digital geometric pattern

Silk scarf design portraying a koi pond on a symbolic circle shaped base

SHIRO BEKKO

2020

Black pigment fineliner, watercolour, digital geometric pattern

Repeated pattern for Café Costume based on 'Koi Pond Circle Japan'

JUST KEEP SWIMMING

2021

Watercolour pencils

Series of repeated patterns of sea life motifs

JUST KEEP SWIMMING

2021

Watercolour pencils, digital water pattern

Panel print with sea life animals

JUST KEEP SWIMMING

2021

Watercolour pencils, digital water pattern

Silk scarf design with shells and sea life motifs

FLOWERY GARDEN POND WITH BIG KOI

2019

Black pigment fineliner, digital drawings, digital colouring techniques

Silk scarf design where the idea of swirling water is replaced by large flowers

SWINGING MONKEYS

2020

Gouache paint, watercolour, digital drawings

Silk scarf design with naively drawn foliage and moving monkeys

JUNGLE BIRDS

2018

Gouache paint, digital border pattern

Silk scarf design based on a hidden archive of vintage stuffed birds

PARADISE JUNGLE

2020

Gouache paint, digital drawings, black pigment fineliner

Detail of a pocket square design for Café Costume based on 'Jungle Birds'

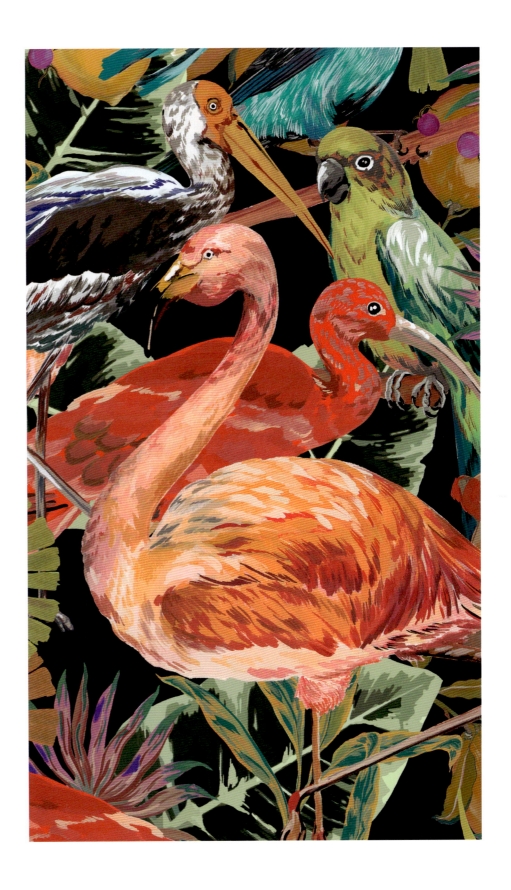

JUNGLE BIRDS AND FLAMINGO

2020

Gouache paint, digitally enhanced

Repeated pattern based on 'Jungle Birds' with parrots

FLAMINGO TOILE

2021

Black pigment fineliner, digital colouring techniques

Modern interpretation of the classic exotic Toile de Jouy style

PARROTS, LILLIES AND FRUIT

2020

Gouache paint, digital leopard pattern

Two parrots surrounded by large painted lilies in a square silk scarf design

FOREST ANIMALS

2020

Black pigment fineliner

Composition of hand drawn forest animals for a square silk scarf design

TILES, BIRDS AND POPPIES

2019

Black pigment fineliner, digital geometric patterns

Silk scarf design taking inspiration from Toile de Jouy and Portuguese tiles

BUTTERFLY IKAT

2020

Digital drawing

An Ikat carpet pattern is mixed with butterflies in magenta and red tones

FOLK BIRDS AND LEMONS

2021

Permanent markers

Inspired by American folk art, using simple markers to accentuate this

BUTTERFLY GARDEN AT NIGHT

2018

Digital drawing

Playful approach to the garden theme with freely drawn plants and insects

BUTTERFLY GARDEN WITH WAVY BORDER

2019

Digital drawing

Oblong silk cotton scarf design based on 'Butterfly Garden at Night'

BUTTERFLY GARDEN WITH KOI

2019

Gouache paint, black pigment fineliner, digital drawing, digital swirl pattern

Bringing many different prints together, creating tension between techniques

BUTTERFLY GARDEN RAINBOW

2019

Digital drawing

Repeated pattern based on 'Butterfly Garden at Night'

POND WITH SWIRLING FISH AND SNAKE

2017

Gouache, watercolour, digital drawing, digital patterns

Silk scarf design where rippling water takes centre stage

MARBLED WATER KOI POND

2019

Gouache paint, black pigment fineliner, digital colouring techniques

Repeated pattern based on 'Flowery Garden Pond with Big Koi'

BUTTERFLY LANDSCAPE

2020

Digital drawing, digital dot pattern

Repeated pattern, taking inspiration from 'Butterfly Garden at Night'

WHITE TIGERS IN A POND SCENE

2020

Black pigmented fineliner, digital drawings

White tigers appear in a pond scene, surrounded by lilies and dragonflies

WHITE TIGERS RAINBOW

2021

Black pigmented fineliner, digital colouring techniques

Repeated pattern based on 'White Tigers in a Pond Scene', with rainbow outlines

PEONIES AND SNAKES

2020

Gouache paint, digital stripe pattern

An experiment with layering existing motifs and patterned structures

LILLY POND

2020

Digital drawing

Repeated pattern depicting a pond scene, using incorrect lilies on purpose

WHITE TIGERS RASPBERRY

2021

Black pigmented fineliner, digital colouring techniques

Small repeated pattern of white tigers in raspberry tones

WHITE TIGERS INDIAN CARPET

2020

Black pigmented fineliner, digital colouring techniques

Looking at historic Asian textiles to rework 'White Tigers' into a blanket design

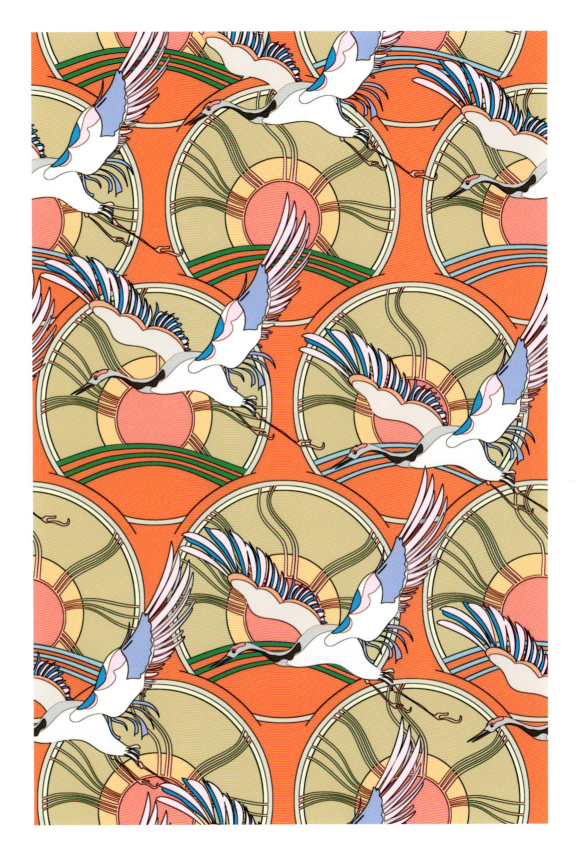

RETRO CRANE BIRDS

2021

Digital drawing

Repeated pattern in a classic repeating manner, outlined for a retro sports feel

CRANE BIRD AND RISING SUN

2020

Digital drawing

Detail of the original repeated pattern, depicting a landscape and crane birds

CRANE BIRD AND RISING SUN

2020

Digital drawing

Complete design for a silk kaftan, adding a geometric border

CRANE BIRDS IN A CLOUDY SKY

2021

Watercolour, digital drawing

Repeated pattern where peonies create the idea of a cloudy, dreamy sky

FOREST BIRDS

2021

Gouache paint

Silk scarf design taking inspiration from archetypal European forest birds

HORSE RACING

2021

Gouache paint, digital drawings

Pocket square design where the paint strokes are as dynamic as the horses

SNAKES AND TULIPS

2019

Gouache paint, digital drawing

Repeated pattern, taking inspiration from the Rijksmuseum artworks

DACHSHUND PENCIL SKETCHES

2021

Pencil

Silk scarf design of mixed pencil sketches, using its negative as a background

FASHION GIRLS AND THEIR DOXIES

2019

Digital drawing

Silk scarf design depicting busy fashion girls walking their little friends

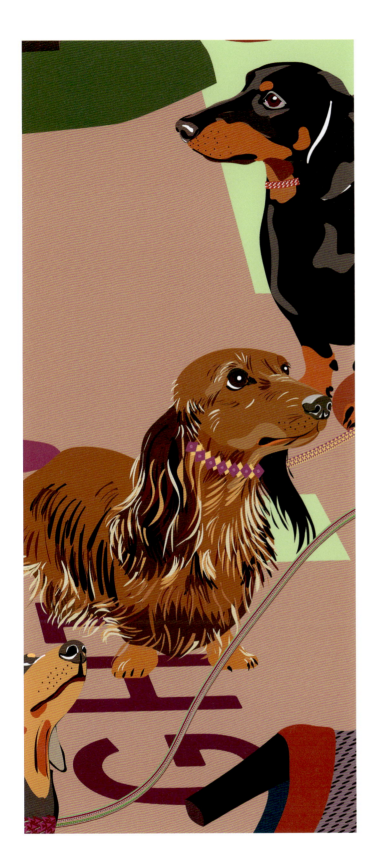

DACHSHUNDS ON LEASHES

2019

Digital drawings, digital dots pattern

Pocket square design based on the orginal 'Fashion Girls and their Doxies'

POODLES AND DACHSHUNDS

2018

Gouache paint, coloured pencils, digital borders, floor and wallpaper pattern

Silk scarf design, using the 'Parrots' pattern as a wallpaper design

PARROT PRINT

2018

Digital drawing

Repeated pattern with multicolour parrots and striped lilies

Flowers & Foliage

Floral patterns always offer an opportunity for a colourful and innocent injection of femininity. Easily read as a safe subject, yet secretly rewarding because of their sensual lines and textures. Step into a wild garden of gouache painted flowers, or sense the naivety in a marker sketched leaf.

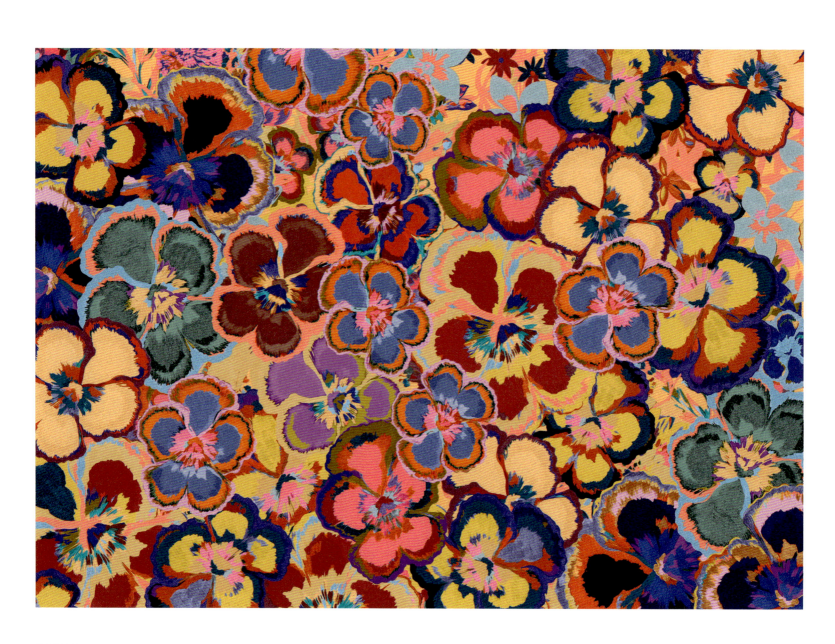

PANSIES

2020

Gouache paint, digitally enhanced

Repeated pattern based on the silk scarf design 'My Dream Garden'

MY DREAM GARDEN

2018

Gouache paint, digital border patterns

Silk scarf design depicting a wild garden full of colour

BRUSH STROKE FLORAL

2021

Gouache paint, black ink

Repeated pattern

PETRYKIVKA FLOWERS

2020

Gouache paint, digitally enhanced

Taking inspiration from a traditional Eastern European painting technique

TULIPS AND WOBBLY STRIPES
2019
Digitalized gouache paint, digital line pattern
Repeated pattern

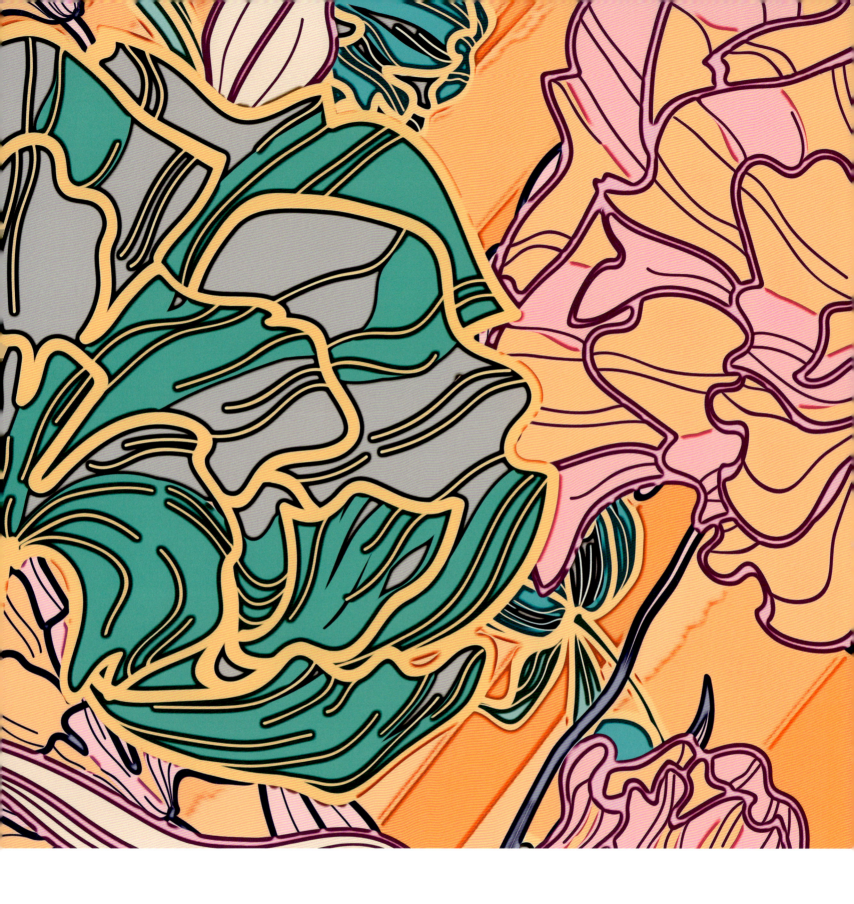

GRAFFITI FLOWERS

2019

Digital drawing

Scarf design using graffiti elements as inspiration to draw abstract flowers

HYDRANGEAS

2020

Gouache paint

Hand painted hydrangeas are puzzled and layed out for this silk scarf design

VINTAGE FRACTURED FLOWERS PLAID

2019

Digital drawing, digital line pattern

Repeated pattern of fractured structures and Liberty-inspired small flowers

PINEAPPLE FEELINGS

2020

Gouache paint, digitally outlined

Repeated pattern resonating with the exotic fruit, without displaying any of it

FEMININITY FLORAL

2021

Digital drawing, watercolour layers

Details of a floral print focusing on female power and blossoming personalities

BLOSSOMING MULTICOLOUR WARM

2021

Gouache paint, digitally enhanced structures

Large hand painted flowers put in a repeated pattern for a car wrap

LARGE RETRO FLOWERS

2021

Digital drawing

Repeated pattern where arched lines and clashing block colours take the centre stage

POPPY FIELD WAVY LEAVES

2021

Digital drawing

Repeated pattern of the original 'Poppy Field' silk scarf design

STRIPED LILIES

2018

Digital drawing

Colour plays the biggest role in this very simply drawn pattern

POPPY FIELD

2021

Digital drawing

Silk scarf design where a wavy border takes inspiration from the poppy leaves

TINY PANSIES

2018

Digital drawing

Repeated pattern with scattered colourful pansies, naively sketched

RETRO FLOWERS JAPAN

2021

Digital drawing

Silk scarf design with typical retro flower drawings, hinting to Japanese prints

POPPY FIELD STRIPED

2021

Digital drawing

Grass halms serve as a border in this silk scarf design

MIKADO FLOWERS

2021

Digital drawing

Repeated pattern of flowers reminding us of a game of Mikado

ART DECO LINE FLORAL

2020

Digital drawing

Repeated pattern based on a series of vintage Art Deco textile patterns

DREAMY LANDSCAPE

2018

Digital drawing

Bouncing around a different planet in this silk scarf design

JUNGLE LANDSCAPE

2020

Digital drawing

Panel print featuring abstract leaves and large rocks

LARGE FLORAL

2019

Digital drawing

Blown up flowers from Flowery Garden Pond with Big Koi for a large scarf

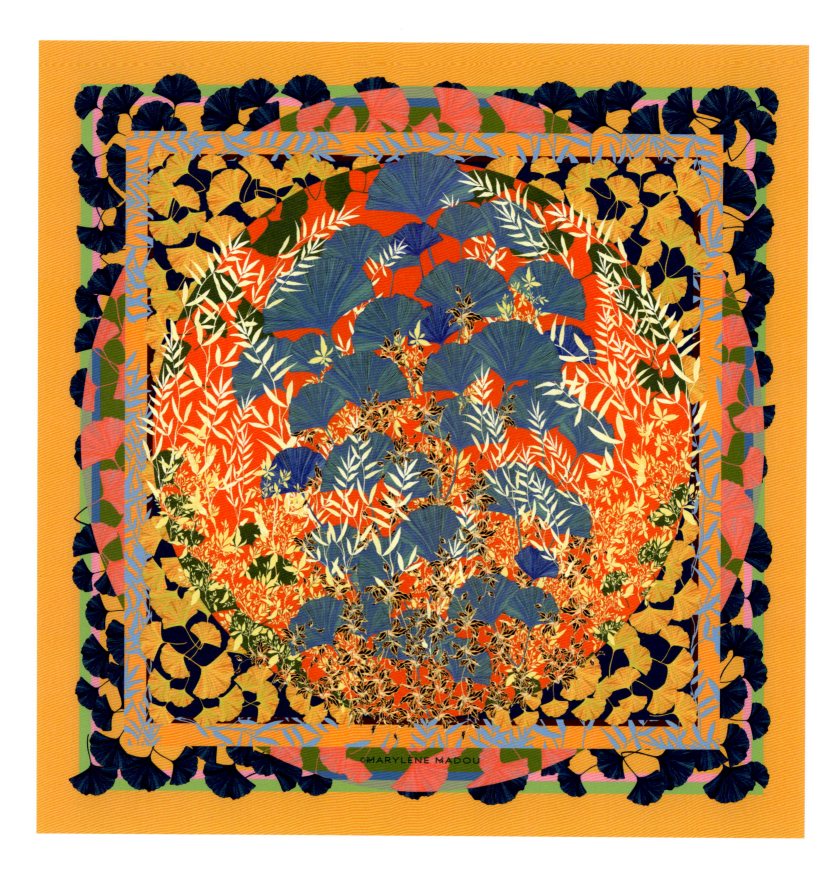

GINKGO CIRCLE JAPAN

2017

Watercolour, gouache paint

Silk scarf design where a circle base is used referencing Japanese symbol design

SUNNY FLOWERS

2018

Watercolour, digitally enhanced

A watercolour painting gets a double exposure effect for a silk scarf design

MARKER FLORALS

2020

Permanent markers

Repeated pattern created for JBC

DITSY BROWN AND GREEN

2019

Permanent markers, digital dot pattern

Repeated pattern with flowers hand drawn with markers

DITSY BLUE AND PETROL

2020

Permanent markers

Repeated pattern created for JBC

Fruits & Vegetables

The tropical, the strange and the exotic. Fruits can look delicious, yet sometimes peculiar and somewhat freakishly with their unconventional shapes, structures and wavy leaves. This in combination with their often bright and overflowing colours makes it the perfect drawable object.

A DREAMY LEMON TREE

2019

Gouache paint, digital border patterns, digital graffiti spray

Silk scarf design based on colourful dreams and other dimensions

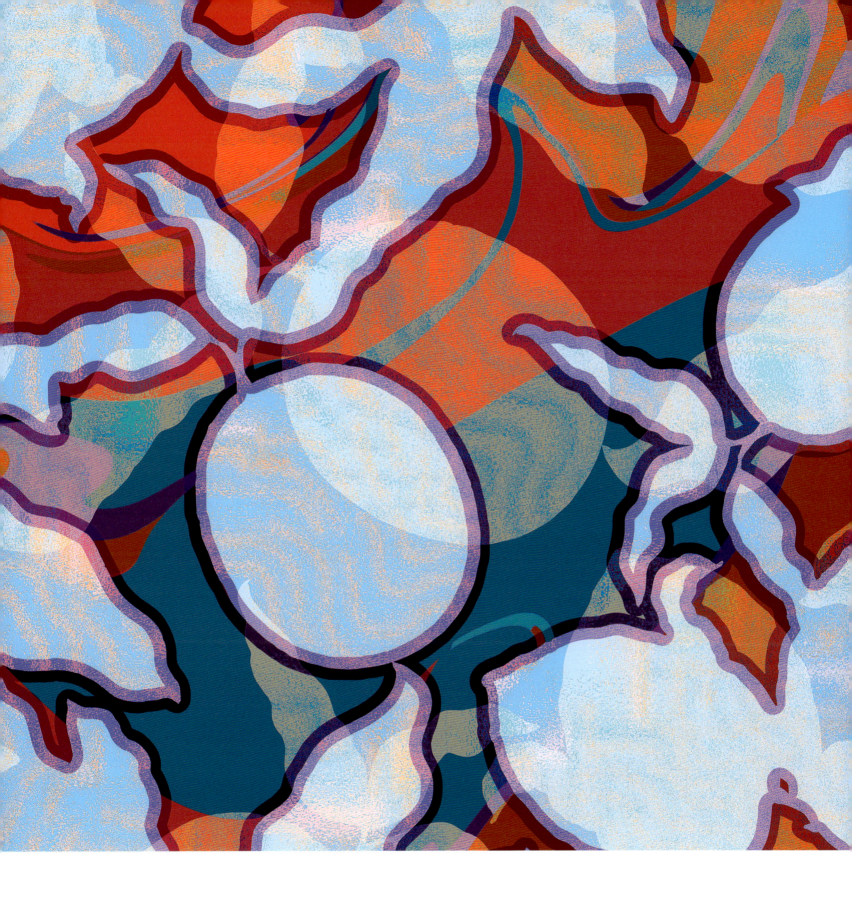

EXOTIC FRUITS AND WAVY LINES

2018

Gouache paint, digital wavy lines pattern

A geometric and organic repeated pattern is layered to enhance one another

EXOTIC FRUITS AND WAVY LINES

2019

Gouache paint, digital wavy lines pattern, digital colouring techniques

Reworked version of the original pattern, taking inspiration from collaging

INKY LEMONS

2020

Ink, digital drawing

Repeated pattern using original ink drawings and digitally drawn elements

CERAMIC FRUITS

2021

Gouache paint, watercolour, digitally enhanced

Repeated pattern for Mayerline, inspired by hand painted Provence pottery

YELLOW PEPPERS AND TOMATOES

2020

Gouache paint

Repeated pattern for JBC using original gouache paintings of tomatoes and peppers

SUPERMARKET FRUIT

2019

Digital drawing

Square scarf design taking inspiration from supermarket fruit displays

SUNFLOWERS, STRAWBERRIES AND HOT PEPPERS

2020

Black pigmented fineliner, digital colouring techniques

Repeated pattern using original ink pen drawings, coloured digitally

PEPPER PLANTS

2020

Digital drawing

Repeated pattern of digitally drawn peppers and a mythical looking plant

FORGOTTEN FRUITS AND VEGETABLES

2021

Pencil

Repeated pattern of cut out sketches on tracing paper for Liane Castermans

VINTAGE STRAWBERRIES

2019

Digital drawing

Silk scarf design inspired by fruit designs on vintage towels and table cloths

Objects & People

Prints and patterns including objects, things and individuals,
easily tell you a story. Seeing a group of fashionable ladies pass
by on the street, booking a holiday to the south, maybe trying
on your favourite pair of shoes? Inspiration is everywhere.

OLD PORT OF NICE

2021

Digital drawing

Repeated pattern inspired by colourful little boats in the port of Nice

STROLLING IN CANNES

2021

Mixed media

Repeated pattern depiciting typical views when visiting Cannes

FASHION GIRLS

2021

Digital drawing

Repeated pattern, depicting fashion girls and flowers

GREEK STATUES

2019

Permanent markers

Silk scarf design taking inspiration from ancient Greek statues

LA BOTTEGA

2021

Digital drawing

Repeated pattern for La Bottega, depicting shoes and accessories

STREETSTYLE DOGS

2020

Black ink, watercolour, permanent markers

Repeated pattern created from original sketches of women walking their dogs

JOCHEN LEËN MARBLE CORAL

2018

Digital drawings

Silk scarf design for jewellery designer Jochen Leën

JOCHEN LEËN FUCHSIA GREEN
2018
Digital drawings
Silk scarf design for jewellery designer Jochen Leën

Abstract & Geometric

Lines, shapes, structures. A building, a technical drawing, a
modern work of art. Just a simple combination of flowing colours.
Abstract prints can be boring and interesting at the same time.

MARBLES

2017

Digital drawing

A game of marbles inspired this square design for a silk scarf

MY SEVENTIES CURTAINS

2019

Digital drawing

Repeated pattern printed on velvet curtains

SWIRLING

2019

Digital drawing

Silk scarf design taking inspiration from the 2017 design Marbles

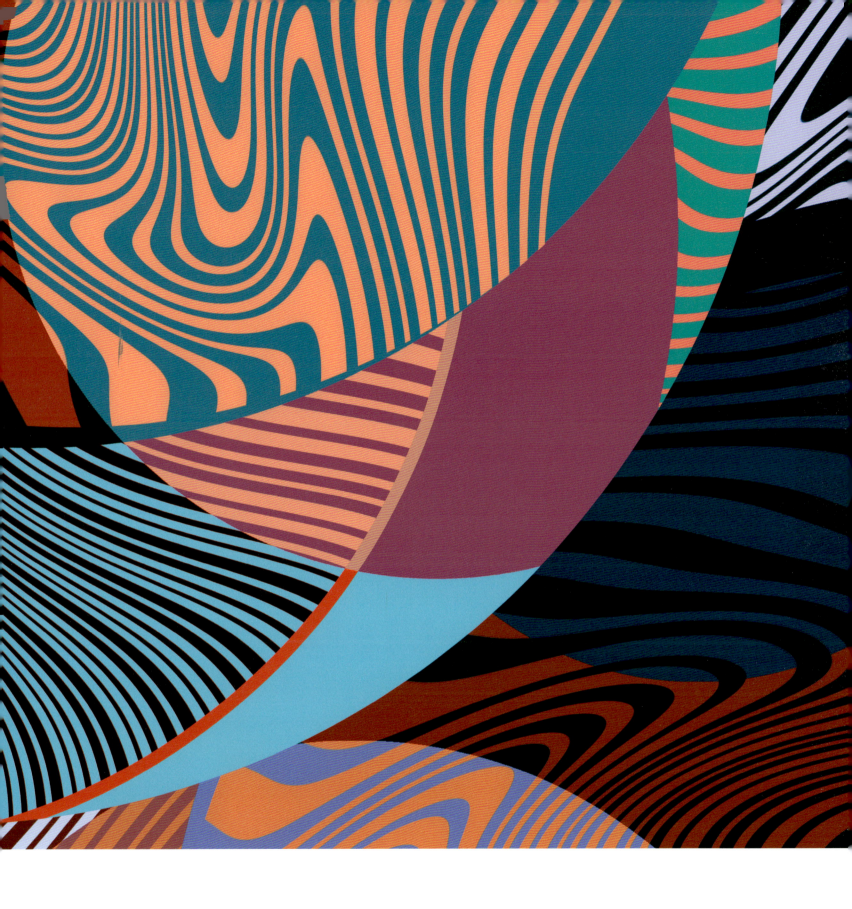

MARBLY WATERS
2018
Digital drawing
A classic marble pattern reinvented in strong contrasting colours

FRACTURED FLORAL

2019

Digital drawing

Silk scarf design layering abstract pieces of flowers and the original Maze print

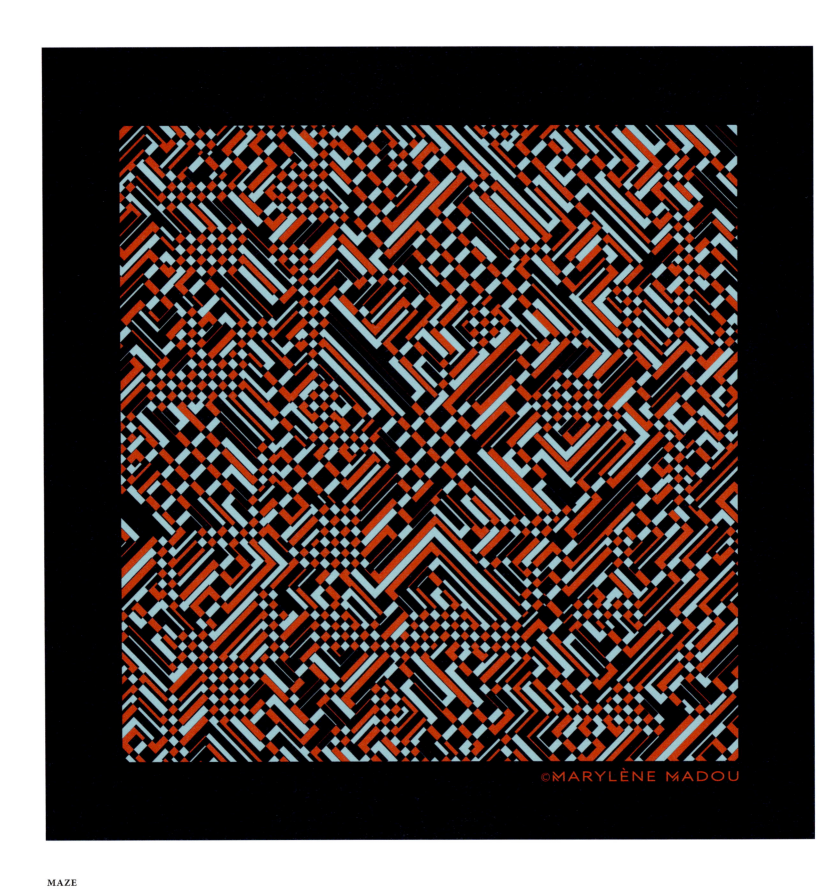

MAZE

2017

Digital drawing

Pocket square design taking inspiration from circuit boards

COBALT CIRCLE MAZE

2017

Digital drawing

Pocket square design inspired by circuit boards

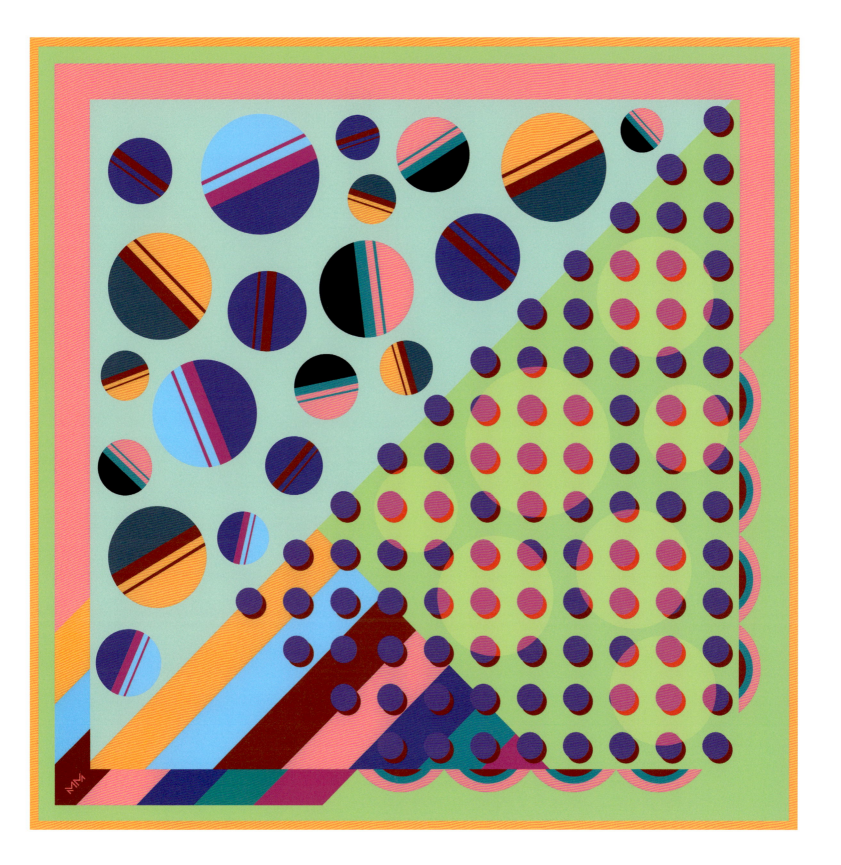

DOTTED DOTS

2018

Digital drawing

Silk scarf design inspired by seventies sportswear details

SUI HANDKERCHIEF

2015

Digital drawing

Square design for a cotton handkerchief based on tower blocks

SUI HANDKERCHIEF

2015

Digital drawing

Square design for a cotton handkerchief inspired by colour fragmentation

COLOURED PENCIL LINES

2019

Digital drawing

Pocket square design where imitated coloured pencil sketches are layered

WOOLY

2020

Digital drawing

Imitated fuzzyness of a wool scarf in a plaid pattern for a cotton handkerchief

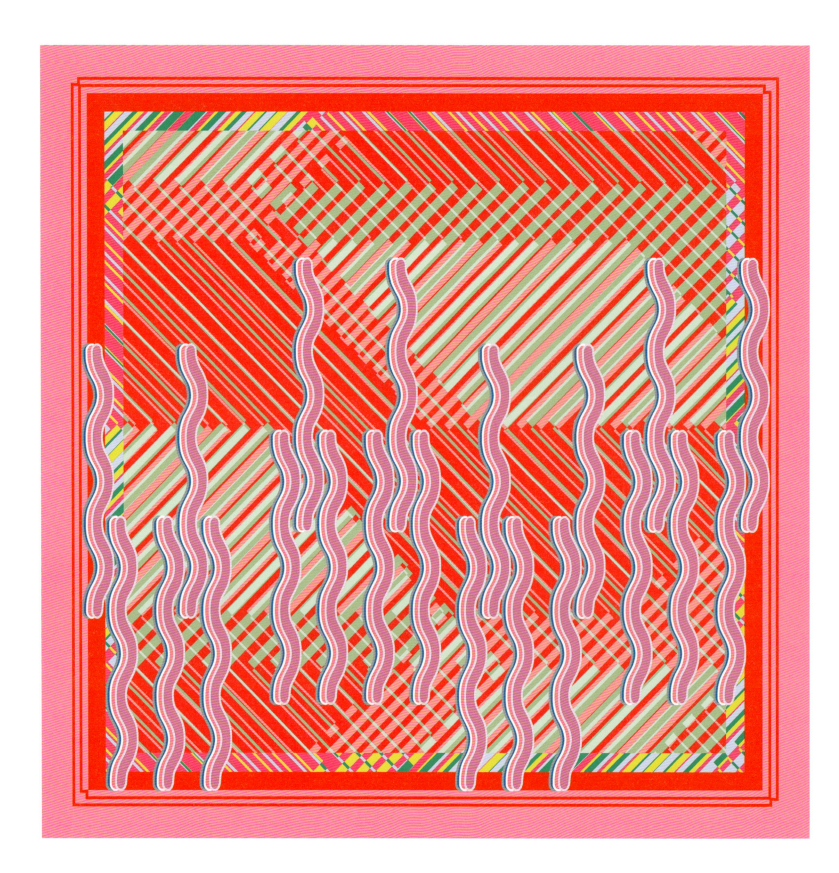

WAVY SITUATION

2018

Digital drawing

Wavy lines and layered geometric line patterns meet for a silk scarf design

GOUFFRE

2020

Digital drawing

Silk scarf design depicting a graphic interpration of a sinkhole and explosion

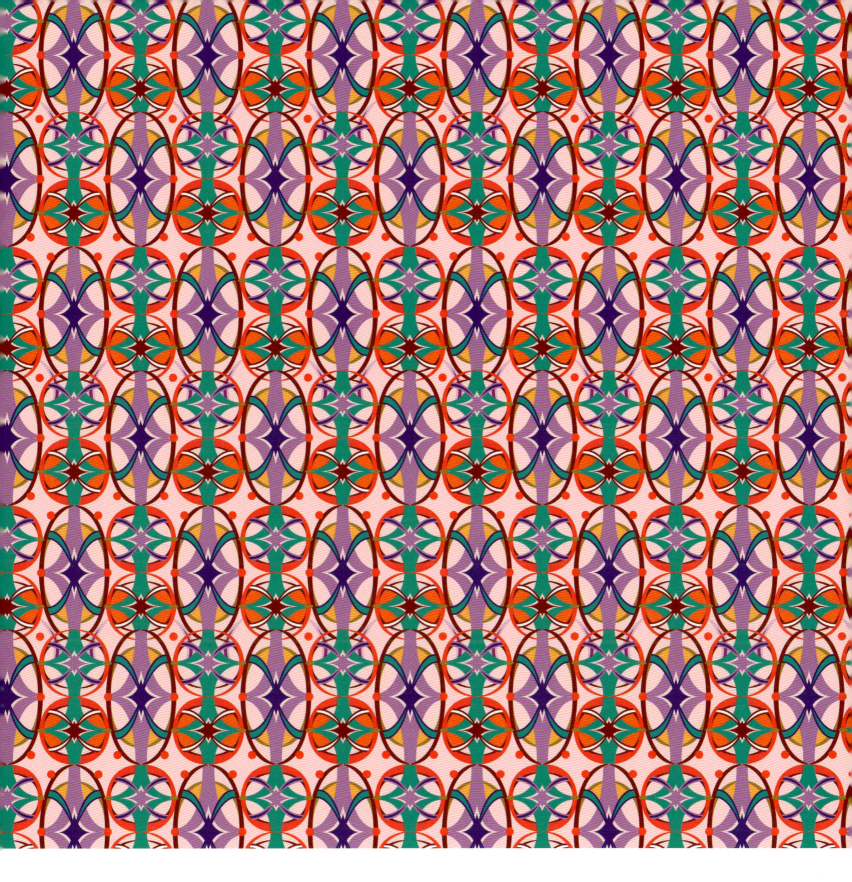

ART DECO DOTS

2020

Digital drawing

Repeated pattern for JBC

MIXED TILES GREEN PINK

2019

Digital drawing

Repeated pattern based on the original silk scarf design 'Mixed Tiles'

MIXED TILES

2020

Digital drawing

Silk scarf design taking inspiration from Portuguese tiles

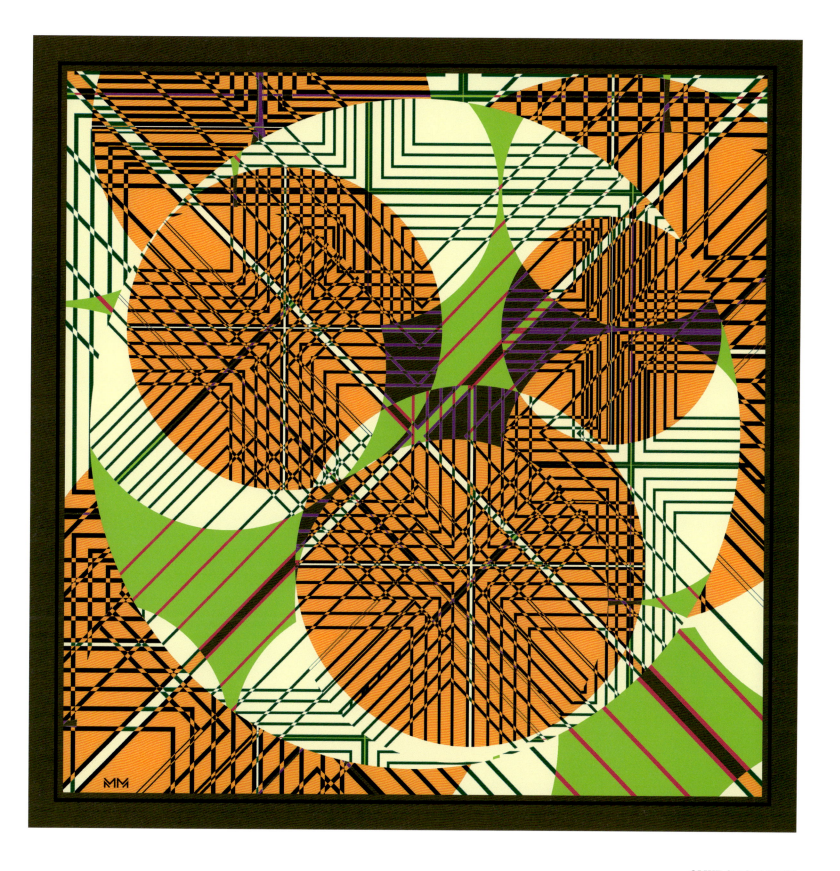

OLIVE CIRCLE MAZE

2018

Digital drawing

Pocket square design taking inspiration from circuit boards

MIXED TILES SOFT MINT

2019

Digital drawing

Cotton handkerchief design based on the original silk scarf design 'Mixed Tiles'

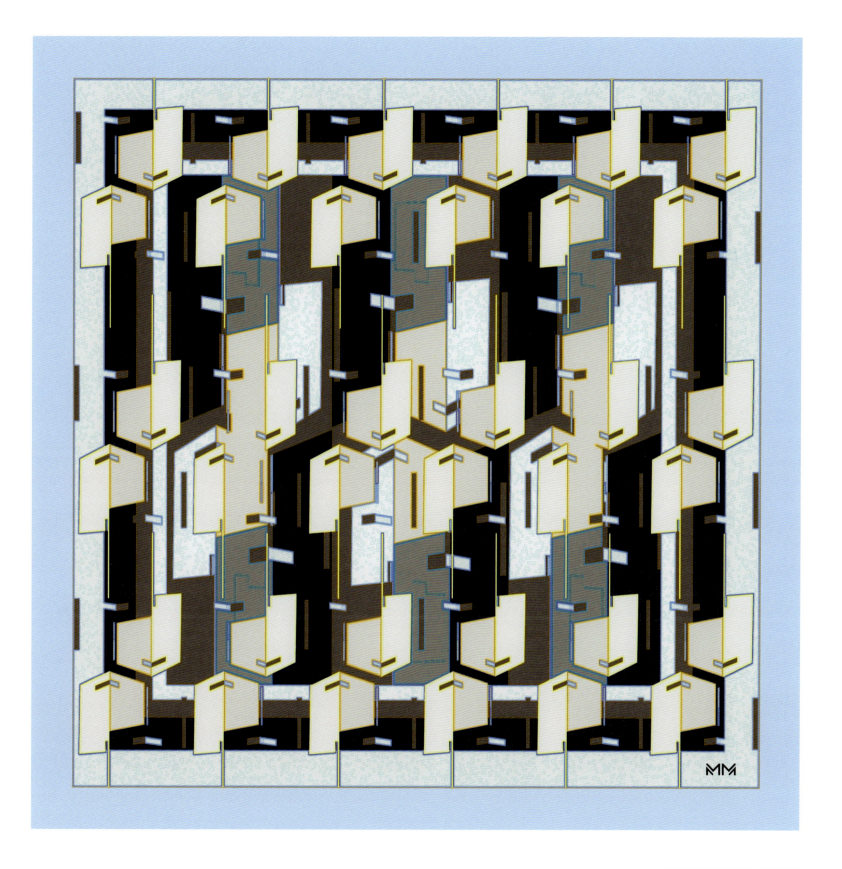

ARCHITECTURAL BLOCKS

2017

Digital drawing

Pocket square design taking inspiration from big city appartment blocks

AZTEC CARPET

2018

Digital drawing

Repeated pattern taking inspiration from Aztec patterns and Ikat carpets

ABSTRACT LEOPARD

2019

Digital drawing

Abstract and organic patterns are layered for this large scarf design

Acknowledgements

Pieces of printed silk cluttering up my desk. A half-finished drawing finds its permanent spot on the corner of the dining table. Books piling up on the TV cabinet, creating an improvised library with several series of the exact same second-hand animal encyclopedias. Without me noticing, creating prints became my daily life.

It was a Kimono in the *Metropolitan Museum of Art* in New York that unexpectedly triggered me as a young girl to explore the world of Asian prints. An internship in Los Angeles at an international print studio taught me the first techniques in turning my analogue drawings into digital textile prints. It turned out to be the beginning of an endlessly growing archive of repeating patterns and placement prints. Unsure wether to call it art, design, or craftsmanship, I fully embraced this newfound passion for a unique skill.

After these first years of research and experimentation, I found it was time for a reference book, an enchiridion so to speak, which highlights the beginning of an archive that today counts hundreds of prints.

I met book designer Tina De Souter, who designed this book so incredibly beautifully, and with her knowledge and expertise, gave the prints their rightful place in a way I could never have imagined. In particular, I would like to thank the inspirer of art books in Belgium, Bruno Devos. His guidance proved invaluable to this project, and details were never overlooked.

Thank you, Oliver, for the opportunity I was given as a young woman, the opportunity which allows me to practice the art of creating digital prints every day now.

Special thanks to Brecht, my life partner, who has supported me not only through this project, and who fully understands the meaning of what is "creating the perfect print" to me.

And my gratitude to you, the reader, the supporter, the backer. Without you, the spectator, there is no visual work of art.

—*Marylène*

Des morceaux de soie imprimée encombrent mon bureau. Un dessin à moitié terminé trouve sa place permanente sur le coin de la table à manger. Les livres s'empilent sur le meuble TV, créant une bibliothèque improvisée avec plusieurs séries des mêmes encyclopédies animalières d'occasion. Sans que je m'en rende compte, la création d'estampes est devenue mon quotidien.

C'est un kimono exposé au *Metropolitan Museum of Art* de New York qui, de manière inattendue, a déclenché chez la jeune fille que je suis l'envie d'explorer le monde des estampes asiatiques. Un stage à Los Angeles dans un atelier d'impression international m'a appris les premières techniques pour transformer mes dessins analogiques en impressions textiles numériques. C'était le début d'une archive sans cesse croissante de motifs répétitifs et d'impressions de tissu. Ne sachant pas si je devais appeler cela de l'art, du design ou de l'artisanat, j'ai pleinement adhéré à cette nouvelle passion pour ce savoir-faire unique.

Après ces premières années de recherche et d'expérimentation, je me suis rendue compte qu'il était temps de créer un livre de référence, un enchiridion pour ainsi dire, qui marquerait le point de départ d'une archive qui compte aujourd'hui des centaines d'impressions.

J'ai rencontré la conceptrice de livres, Tina De Souter, qui a conçu ce livre d'une manière incroyablement belle et qui, grâce à ses connaissances et à son expertise, a donné aux estampes la place qui leur revient d'une manière que je n'aurais jamais imaginée. Je tiens à remercier tout particulièrement l'inspirateur des livres d'art en Belgique, Bruno Devos. Ses conseils se sont avérés inestimables pour ce projet, et aucun détail n'a jamais été négligé.

Merci, Oliver, pour l'opportunité qui m'a été donnée en tant que jeune femme, opportunité qui me permet aujourd'hui de pratiquer chaque jour l'art de créer des impressions numériques.

Un merci spécial à Brecht, mon partenaire de vie, qui m'a soutenu non seulement à travers ce projet, et qui comprend parfaitement la signification de ce que « créer l'impression parfaite » pour moi.

Et ma gratitude envers vous, le lecteur, le supporter, le mécène. Sans vous, le spectateur, il n'y a pas d'œuvre d'art visuel.

VINTAGE FRACTURED FLOWERS
PLAID P. 85

POODLES AND DACHSHUNDS P. 70

BUTTERFLY GARDEN WITH KOI P. 37

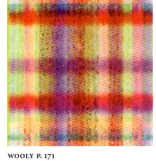

WOOLY P. 171

WHITE TIGERS RAINBOW P. 47

PARROT PRINT P. 71

WHITE TIGERS RASPBERRY P. 52

BUTTERFLY GARDEN WITH WAVY
BORDER P. 36

BUTTERFLY LANDSCAPE P. 44

ART DECO LINE FLORAL P. 102

WAVY SITUATION P. 172

BLOSSOMING MULTICOLOUR WARM P. 90

WHITE TIGERS IN A POND SCENE P. 46

MARBLY WATERS P. 161

AZTEC CARPET P. 182

POND WITH SWIRLING FISH AND
SNAKE P. 41

MIKADO FLOWERS P. 101

LILLY POND P. 50

EXOTIC FRUITS AND WAVY LINES P. 122

BUTTERFLY IKAT P. 31

PARROTS, LILLIES AND FRUIT P. 27

GRAFFITI FLOWERS P. 83

RETRO CRANE BIRDS P. 55

SNAKES AND TULIPS P. 64

STREETSTYLE DOGS P. 149

A DREAMY LEMON TREE P. 118

MY DREAM GARDEN P. 75

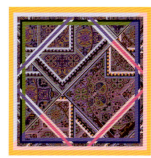

MIXED TILES P. 178

MY SEVENTIES CURTAINS P. 156

TULIPS AND WOBBLY STRIPES P. 81

GINKGO CIRCLE JAPAN P. 110

BUTTERFLY GARDEN AT NIGHT P. 34

VINTAGE STRAWBERRIES P. 134

PANSIES P. 74

PEONIES AND SNAKES P. 49

POPPY FIELD WAVY LEAVES P. 93

CERAMIC FRUITS P. 124

FOREST BIRDS P. 60

DACHSHUNDS ON LEASHES P. 69

WHITE TIGERS INDIAN CARPET P. 53

MAZE P. 165

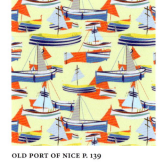

OLD PORT OF NICE P. 139

POPPY FIELD STRIPED P. 99

BRUSH STROKE FLORAL P. 79

STROLLING IN CANNES P. 140

FEMININITY FLORAL P. 88

YELLOW PEPPERS AND TOMATOES P. 126

JOCHEN LEËN FUCHSIA GREEN P. 151

PEPPER PLANTS P. 131

SUNNY FLOWERS P. 111

PETRYKIVKA FLOWERS P. 80

FORGOTTEN FRUITS AND VEGETABLES P. 133

PINEAPPLE FEELINGS P. 87

SUPERMARKET FRUIT P. 127

JOCHEN LEËN MARBLE CORAL P. 150

JUST KEEP SWIMMING P. 11

OLIVE CIRCLE MAZE P. 179

SUI HANDKERCHIEF P. 169

FEMININITY FLORAL P. 89

LARGE RETRO FLOWERS P. 92

SWINGING MONKEYS P. 18

JUNGLE BIRDS P. 20

HORSE RACING P. 62

MARBLES P. 154

PARADISE JUNGLE P. 21

FASHION GIRLS AND THEIR DOXIES P. 68

MARBLED WATER KOI POND P. 42

MIXED TILES SOFT MINT P. 180

DACHSHUND PENCIL SKETCHES P. 66

JUST KEEP SWIMMING P. 14

POPPY FIELD P. 96

MIXED TILES GREEN PINK P. 176

CRANE BIRD AND RISING SUN P. 56

DITSY BLUE AND PETROL P. 115

JUNGLE LANDSCAPE P. 105

JUST KEEP SWIMMING P. 10

DOTTED DOTS P. 167

LARGE FLORAL P. 108

DREAMY LANDSCAPE P. 104

FASHION GIRLS P. 143

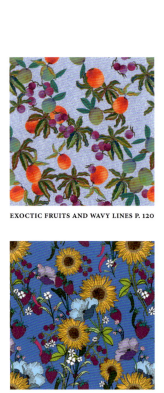

EXOCTIC FRUITS AND WAVY LINES P. 120

HYDRANGEAS P. 84

MARKER FLORALS P. 112

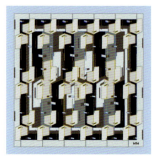

ARCHITECTURAL BLOCKS P. 181

SUNFLOWERS, STRAWBERRIES AND HOT PEPPERS P. 129

FLAMINGO TOILE P. 26

GOUFFRE P. 174

FOREST ANIMALS P. 28

RETRO FLOWERS JAPAN P. 98

JUST KEEP SWIMMING P. 12

GREEK STATUES P. 144

CRANE BIRDS IN A CLOUDY SKY P. 58

KOI POND CIRCLE JAPAN P. 8

INKY LEMONS P. 123

FLOWERY GARDEN POND WITH BIG KOI P. 17

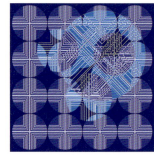

COBALT CIRCLE MAZE P. 166

BUTTERFLY GARDEN RAINBOW P. 38

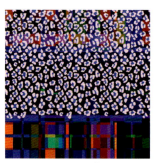

FRACTURED FLORAL P. 162

ABSTRACT LEOPARD P. 183

MAZE P. 164

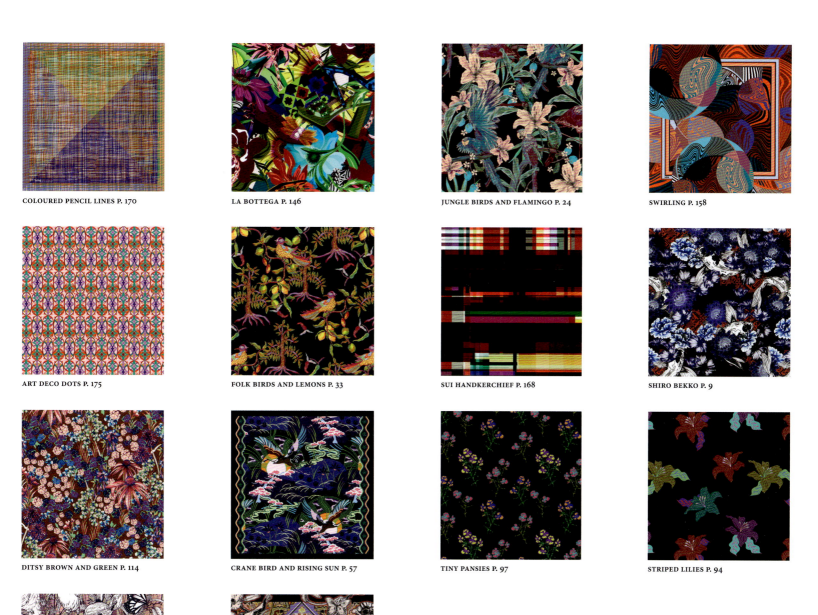

COLOURED PENCIL LINES P. 170

LA BOTTEGA P. 146

JUNGLE BIRDS AND FLAMINGO P. 24

SWIRLING P. 158

ART DECO DOTS P. 175

FOLK BIRDS AND LEMONS P. 33

SUI HANDKERCHIEF P. 168

SHIRO BEKKO P. 9

DITSY BROWN AND GREEN P. 114

CRANE BIRD AND RISING SUN P. 57

TINY PANSIES P. 97

STRIPED LILIES P. 94

FOREST ANIMALS P. 29

TILES, BIRDS AND POPPIES P. 30

Prints & Patterns

© 2021 Stockmans Art Books & Marylène Madou

Illustrations & prints: Marylène Madou
www.marylenemadou.com

Published by: Bruno Devos at Stockmans Art Books
www.stockmansartbooks.be

Book Design: Tina De Souter
www.tinadesouter.be

Text: Sofie Gielis

Copywriting: Femke Vanhoutte
www.thespotlightagency.be

Printed by: Stockmans at Antilope De Bie Printing

Printed in a first edition of 700 copies, December 2021

ISBN: 9789077207994
Legal Deposit: D/2021/09816/16